Raising Your Teenage Daughter:

A Guide to Curbing the Rebel

Table of Contents

Introduction: Why you need this book

Part 1. Playing the Long Game: Your Vision for Your Daughter

Part 2. Ten Simple Rules for Talking to Your Teenager
- 1. Listen
- 2. Be transparent about your feelings
- 3. Remember, it's a conversation
- 4. This is not a battle
- 5. She's a *person*
- 6. Pick your moments for the heavy conversations
- 7. Draw the line on attitude
- 8. Ruin her life!
- 9. Good times
- 10. Be patient - it's a long game

Part 3. Five Common Conflicts and How to Handle Them
- 1. Friends, peer pressure and social media
- 2. Clothes
- 3. Relationships
- 4. School work
- 5. Chores

The Other Side of the Teenage Years

Introduction: Why read this book?

First of all, you need to get your mindset right. This is your daughter we're talking about, not an evil monster or an enemy you must conquer in a battle! It's easy to lose perspective on this because such a barrage of negativity surrounds us when it comes to this topic. People like to vent their frustration about the difficulties they face in raising teen girls, and they have every right to; it can be a harrowing experience. But because of this, we can sometimes forget the bigger picture and lose sight of the small victories and glimmers of hope that shine through when it comes to our daughters. This guide will help you to look out for those special moments, refresh your thinking, take a practical approach and help you take a step back from the rollercoaster of the teenage years.

There are many publications out there about how to raise teenage girls, so why should you read this one? Well, firstly, this guide is aimed at parents who feel overwhelmed with the amount of information that we have access to on this topic. Rest assured, this guide cuts through all the psycho-babble, platitudes, and wishy-washy advice to give you simple truths about the realities of raising teenage girls. Secondly, this is an honest guide that recognizes that perfection is an unrealistic and actually dangerous goal when it comes to parenting and highlights the importance of making mistakes and being flexible in your decision-making. The aim of this book is to empower parents to be the best they can be without making them feel judged, incapable, unworthy or unable to win. After all, you already have a teen daughter who is quite capable of making you feel like that!

Part 1. Playing the Long Game: Your Vision For Your Daughter

When you picture your daughter leaving your care, to go off to college, or to work, travel and strike out on her own, what skills, values and attitudes do you want her to have? How will you prepare her for the kind of life she is likely to live, in terms of work and career, friends, family and relationships, values and morals? These sound like lofty ideals, but it really helps to have a clear picture of what you (and, eventually, she) wants out of life. The teen years are a process by which the responsibility for her hopes and goals transfer from your hands to hers, so it is understandable that these times are ones of rocky transition. The more deliberate you can be about these things, the easier it will be for you to stand firm and draw the boundaries that all teens need (and secretly want). With the long game in mind, the day-to-day struggles, arguments, whinging and so on will be easier to cope with, or at least feel somewhat more purposeful.

You must expect a great deal from your daughter: if you set the bar too low, she won't have anything to strive for. Expect good behaviour, reinforce it, and you will get it (at least some of the time). Expect poor behaviour, and you know what, you will probably get it, and worse. Be clear about your expectations, think about what matters the most and be willing to compromise reasonably and let things go occasionally. For example, good manners might be important to you. Great! But if this is a boundary that she keeps pushing incessantly and that is causing major friction to the point that other problems are arising (such as staying out past curfew because it's so stressful to be at home), and you are in a vicious cycle of arguing and consequences, it might be time to take a step back on that particular issue. Give her some breathing space, let the dynamic 're-set' itself and push beyond the cycle of negativity. You might find that the good manners magically return when you make less of a big deal about it or when she has less of a reason for a 'me against the world' mindset. Remember that, just like when she was a little girl, she needs a win occasionally, so sometimes you need to give her a clean slate in order to 'catch' her doing the right thing.

As hard as it is to come to terms with, a lot of the time when you are raising a teenager, you will feel like you are failing when you are actually succeeding. It can be hard to see the light at the end of the tunnel, especially if this is your first teenager. There is no rhyme or reason to when things start to come together—it can happen quickly or painstakingly slowly, but one way or another, it will happen. Before you know it you will have to start to cope with the difficulties of being a parent to an independent adult!

This idea of feeling like you are failing when you are actually succeeding is very hard to get a handle on. You might feel like: "I enforce all these rules about speaking respectfully, but she still sometimes talks to me in the most abhorrent tone". You might feel like: "I set boundaries around when she should get home at night, or how often she goes online, but she still sneaks around and tries to get away with things". Yes, in the moment, these situations can feel like failure. But think of the alternative situation: You tell your daughter a couple of times to speak to you nicely, and what, she just does it forever more? Or, you impose a curfew of 9 p.m. on weekends, and what, she's always home on the dot? The very idea is laughable!

This is why you need to be clear in your own mind about why each and every one of your rules and expectations for her behaviour are in place. In reality, all of these restrictions are there to keep her safe, to ensure that she is a respectful person (not just to you but to everyone who deserves it) and to give her rights and responsibilities that are equal to her stage of maturity. These rules and expectations are there not so much with the intention that she follows them to the letter 24/7, but rather so that she is knows that she is cared for until such a time that she has the cognitive and emotional ability to do so herself. Pushing these limits and occasionally crossing them is a part of this process, and your role in this process is to consistently enforce the line so that she knows exactly where it is. One day she will be in a world where she draws her own lines and you want her to understand her limits well enough to know where to draw them and when to push them.

For this reason, you should tell her "No" often, but also always tell her why. Even well explained rules and boundaries are toxic to teens, so arbitrary rules are practically lethal. Even if it seems like she is not taking in your reasons for "Why", rest assured that she is on some level. Her pushing against these (reasonable) boundaries is not reason to give up on them, rather it is a good sign that she feels safe in your relationship and wants to grow. A teen that never pushes the boundaries in any way will never strive to achieve and branch out. It is up to you to make sure the boundaries are fair but flexible and allow her opportunities to show that she is maturing and growing up. An added bonus of telling her "Why" is that it will keep you in check as well! Sometimes it is easy to fall into the trap of trying to restrict everything, in a vain attempt to protect her and control her life, but as we all know, if there are too many rules, they will always start to seem unfair and unreasonable. When that happens, even the ones she actually agrees are reasonable might start to seem unduly restrictive. This is a situation to avoid at all costs—rebellion against everything! Therefore, keep the "Why" firmly in mind, and be pragmatic about rule making.

Apart from "No", there's something else you should tell her often as well. I think you know what that is. Tell her that you love her. And again, the same concept above applies here as well: tell her why. Tell her that she is smart, beautiful inside and out, caring, honest, a good friend, a great daughter and an interesting person—she is, even if she isn't showing it to you right now. Many parents of teenagers hear wonderful things about their kids from other parents, teachers, extended family and friends. They truly do save the best of themselves for others during this time. It's up to you to remember this and be aware of the fact that if they are horrible to you, it's because they trust and love you most of all.

Part 2. Ten Simple Rules for Talking to Your Teenage Daughter

So much of dealing with the teenage years is about communication. Sometimes during these turbulent times the lines of communication can be rather stilted, and even blocked off completely. These ten practical, realistic tips will help you to keep the conversation going, even when those moody silences start to plague your relationship.

1. Listen.

The most important thing to remember when talking to teenage girls is actually not about talking at all- it's about listening. Remember when you were that age and it felt like no one cared about your views or struggles? It was very frustrating and made you feel like everyone was against you. So, before you start sharing your wisdom with a teenage girl, as difficult as it is, the first thing you must always do is listen. Most teenage girls will have a lot to say, and even though it might seem like angst-filled ranting to you, it is vital that they feel that they can talk to you about what is going on in their life. This means you might have to hear a lot of "Like, Jenny said to Amber that Clarissa liked Jeff, but, like, Melissa doesn't think so and she likes Ryan anyway" to get to the more relevant insights into your teenager's life, but it is a crucial step in the process. Don't trivialise the small stuff going on in her life, and she will be more willing to come to you with the big stuff.

2. Be transparent about your feelings.

Keeping the communication lines open is a two-way street. You can't expect your daughter to come to the party in terms of information about her life if you never share anything 'real' about yours. This doesn't mean it will be all-talking, all the time—everyone needs their space occasionally. The trick is to not let issues linger. After a 'discussion', fight, or 'World War 15', whatever you want to call it, make sure you always touch base on the problem, even if it is a little ways down the track when things have cooled down. Teenagers hate to feel like they are being brushed aside or that things are being swept under the rug—they see this as the height of hypocrisy.

So tell them when they make you angry, sad or disappointed, and mean it. Tell them in the moment, but also definitely reiterate it later on, when their ears are no longer shut off by anger. Do not shield them from your emotions: they might even help them to remember you're human! That isn't to say that you should offload all of your emotional baggage on them, but don't hide everything from them either. Knowing that adults have feelings and face difficult times is an important part of growing up. Showing them that you face obstacles and involving them in how you overcome them will provide them with insight into how to deal with their own problems. Treat them as an adult-in-training, not as a kid. Some of the most powerful realisations a teenager can have occur as they begin to see their parents as people.

3. Remember, it's a conversation.

No one likes to be lectured to. Oftentimes, by talking to a teenager through an exchange of ideas, rather than just "Here's what you should do", you can prompt them to come to the same conclusion without forcing it on them. The added bonus of this is that they are more likely to understand the 'why' of the situation and will therefore be able to better apply it in different situations in the future. In addition, because they have gone through the thought process behind the decisions or ideas, they will feel ownership of it and, if you're lucky, will feel like they've come up with it all on their own. Sure, it might take an extra twenty minutes of talking together to reach the same point as what you could have told them in a one-minute lecture, but it will be much more effective in the long run.

Also, keep in mind that every conversation is not an opportunity for a life lesson. When the conversation is flowing it might be tempting to ride that wave right on through to the moral of the story. This is a most groan-inducing habit that all parents have. If you can refrain yourself once in a while and enjoy a conversation with you daughter that is a bit frivolous, silly and light-hearted or demonstrates a genuine interest in *her* views, this will go a long way towards her taking the heavy conversations more seriously.

4. *This is not a battle.*

It might feel like it, especially if there's a lot of screaming and then retreating (from both sides), but try as hard as possible to keep from engaging in and seeing this as a kind of warfare. Do not get involved in screaming matches— sure, let them vent (within reason), but no one wins if you both end up in all-out arguments all the time. In an ideal world, these kinds of arguments would never happen, but of course they do. After all, guaranteed no one knows better how to push your buttons than your teenage daughter. Try your best to minimise these kinds of arguments, but when they inevitably do happen, make sure that something good comes out of them in the aftermath when both parties are ready to put forward a treaty.

As an adult, it's easy to think that the life of a teenager is fairly easy: few responsibilities, lots of hanging out with friends, your hopes and dreams not yet crushed by reality, right? But think back—did it actually *feel* that easy? When you think about it, there are a lot of things going on for a teenager, stuck between childhood and adulthood, unsure of how the world works but often expected to act as though they do. Some teens have pressure coming at them from all directions, pressure to "be good in school", "do your chores", "respect your elders", "get into college", "be popular", "be pretty", "get a boyfriend", "don't grow up too fast", "stop acting like a child". This barrage of mixed messages combined with explosive hormones—is it any wonder that she sometimes turns into a monster? Remember to give her a break from all this, don't trivialize her worries and fears and try to understand where she is coming from. This isn't about making excuses—it's about role-modelling empathy and helping her to recognize the root cause of her behaviour.

5. She's a person.

Sometimes in the depth of the teenage years it can be hard to reconcile the little girl you once knew with the ball of emotions you are now confronted with. It might be hard, but you should attempt to stay aware of the fact that the best aspects of that little girl are still in there, and will, with some effort, re-emerge at some point as a fully-formed adult. Mistakes will be made (on your part as well as hers). Once in a while you should own up to your mistakes—this shows her that adults are not infallible, but also that it is important to take responsibility for your actions.

When she makes mistakes (which, again, she will—it's a *crucial* part of the learning process!), do not tell your daughter she is 'bad', or irresponsible, or that she'll never be successful or amount to anything. Yes, these things might be true if she continues with this behaviour. But try to remember to separate her behaviour from who she is as a person—and remind her of this too. Tell her she is strong, smart, caring and all the other virtues you value, even if her behaviour isn't showing it right at that moment. Even if she has done something 'bad', she needs to know that this doesn't define her and be reminded of the person that she wants to be, and that you know she is deep inside. Reinforce the person she wants to be (not the person you want her to be) and she will strive to live up to this view of herself, without being burdened by expectation.

6. Pick your moments for the heavy conversations.

I used to hate it when my parents made a big show of having a serious discussion with me, because it felt like I was being cornered. I would feel panicky and stressed, unsure what was coming or how to react. They always seemed to take so long to get to the point, while I sat their worrying that they were about to drop some kind of horrible bombshell!

Choose your moments, don't make it a big deal (even if it is) and lay it out there: just say it. Don't say vague but alarming things like, "We need to have a talk later". Plan to work things into conversation as naturally as possible, when she is calm and you both have time to talk. A good time to talk can be when you're doing something together, but you have her attention—like driving somewhere, going for a walk, baking some cookies or throwing around a ball. This way, you both have something else to focus on and everything feels a lot less intense. This is a strategy that is often recommended strategy for dealing with teenage boys, but, really, it is just as effective for girls, and in fact most people of all ages. Teen boys don't have the monopoly on monosyllabic answers, after all!

As for those rare and delightful moments when she wants to talk to you (it will happen!), you need to be receptive to this mood and be ready to engage—even if it's not an ideal time for you. Just like how as a toddler she used to always need your attention as soon as you got on the phone or went to the bathroom, now she will be most receptive to talking right when you're settling in to watch your favourite TV show or about to go for a run. These occasions might be rare, so you need to capitalize on them when they happen. Of course this doesn't mean you need to live your life according to the whims of your girl's level of communicativeness on any particular day, but you should make the sacrifice where possible and always follow up with her if you can't.

7. Draw the line on attitude.

The rolling eyes, the entitlement, the sighs, the "But Moooom's"—these are all par for the course. Mostly you can just think of these as window-dressing, as evidence that your girl is growing up but has not yet got the skills to communicate appropriately. Remind her that *how* she talks to people will impact how they will respond. If she asks you for something, rudely, guess what the answer should be? It should be the same answer she would get if she was asking in that way from anyone outside her family: "No". Give her the chance to try again: "Would you like to put that differently?" If she can't make an improvement, show her how. If she *won't* make an improvement, the answer stays, "No" until she can. Don't engage with her when she is showing this kind of attitude and she will quickly learn to curtail it as much as possible. Set this standard and stick to it early and it will save a lot of angst on both sides later. As for stickier points like swearing, that depends on your family's values. Some prefer a zero-tolerance blanket ban. Others don't mind swearing out of anger or frustration as long as it is not directed *at* anyone. Regardless of where the line is for your family, the important thing is that you and she know where it is, and that you stick to the consequences of crossing it.

8. Ruin her life!

If you haven't ruined your teenager's life at least once between the ages of thirteen and eighteen, you are a very lucky parent. "Why are you ruining my life?" is the catchcry of teenage girls everywhere. Their justifications for throwing this one-liner at you would be funny if they didn't reflect such a ridiculously dramatic, petty and self-centred attitude. But rest assured, they don't mean it. Well, maybe they feel like they mean it, but they really don't. When they say this, what they are really saying is: "Why won't you let me do what *I* want?" They can't see the reality of the situation; all they see is unfairness, restrictions and control—that is, their lack of control.

When they throw this at you, your consistent, constant reply must be: "Because I love you". This will frustrate them, no doubt, but it might occasionally help them see things from your point of view, or at least catch a glimpse of this through their rage. If your answer of "I love you" seems ridiculous even to you, then perhaps this particular boundary is one that is worth loosening or re-considering completely.

At the same time, in the never-ending balancing act that is parenthood, remember that you are not meant to be the 'good cop' all the time. Adolescents need a 'bad cop' in their life and as their parent, this unpleasant task will most often fall to you. They won't appreciate it. They may (pretend) to hate you for it. They'll say, "Everyone else's parents let them". But parenting isn't a popularity contest (luckily, or else we'd all be screwed!). Your role is to create rules and boundaries for your teenager that they can safely push against. Without these parentally-imposed boundaries to test, you can guarantee they will find more dangerous and damaging ways to assert their independence. Ruin their life a little now, and there will be less chance that they will ruin their own life when the stakes are higher.

9. Good times.

Make sure there are good times. Cycles of negativity need to be broken. Create good times between you, your teenage daughter/s and the rest of the family, even if you have to manufacture them. Do nice things for them—a little present like some new nail polish, t-shirt or a book every once in a while "just because I love you" will stop things from seeming like a constant battle. This doesn't need to break the bank and shouldn't turn into a constant flow of gifts that will only turn into bribery and result in entitlement. Rather, something small like a little note or a flower on their bed at unexpected moments will do wonders. Also, try to spend some special, one-on-one downtime together—at a movie, a concert, a walk, or a coffee together. Doing something a little grown up or a little ritual that only you do together can provide some nice breathing space. At first it might be awkward, particularly if these are things you don't usually do together. Push through that and it will become the new normal.

Some one-on-one time with Dad or Mom can work wonders—you might even hear a few things that she normally wouldn't tell you with the other one there! If she doesn't have both parents in her life, or relations between her and one or both are particular strained, it might be worth thinking about the other adults in her life—like an aunt or uncle, a trusted neighbor or family friend—who can fulfil this role. Sometimes this happens naturally, but other times you will need to do the arranging behind the scenes.

Don't use your special downtimes with your daughter to initiate big conversations. If they happen naturally, let them, but let her come to you in those moments if she wants. Make these times a safe haven where she can just be and you can both separate from the pressures of the parent-child relationship. Of course there will be occasions where these 'special times' together aren't much fun. By their very nature, teenage girls don't necessarily want to be hanging out with their Mom or Dad. So try to plan it in advance, or make it a regular thing, so that it actually happening doesn't hinge on her behaviour or get cancelled because someone isn't in the mood (either her or you!). Believe me, whether or not she complains about these times, or seems reluctant about them, she will remember them, and treasure them one day in the future.

10. Be patient—it's a long game.

These years are a time for planting seeds that may not come to fruition for many years. In fact, your daughter may never make the connection between things that you tell her or make her do and the kind of person she ends up being! So it truly is a bit of a thankless task of repeating the same lessons until they stick. Despite this, many parents do end up getting a thank you of sorts, when their child grows up and they can finally step back and say, "I did an okay job". Some even luckier parents might hear these (sheepish) words from their child's lips! But don't count on it. Instead, as you have these conversations, make these tough decisions, question yourself, worry, struggle and celebrate the small victories along the way, think of the big picture, your vision for the person your daughter will choose to be and how you can best equip her to fulfil her best self.

Part 3. Five Common Conflicts and How to Handle Them.

1. Friends, peer pressure and social media.

It can be hard to keep up with your teenager's social life, especially when you might suddenly be hearing a lot less about what goes on at school. The days when she was bursting to tell you all her problems at the end of the school day might now seem like a distant memory. This is perfectly natural—all that practice she had finding, making and losing friends as a kid is hopefully helping her now as she moves into new social circles and tries to navigate the complex social hierarchy of teenagers.

This doesn't mean you should give up on being involved though. Try to know her friends. Don't be invasive or try to 'hang out' with them and be 'the cool Mom', but try to keep up-to-date with what's going on in her peer group.

The things she will be willing to tell you will most likely be selective (i.e. the less scandalous stuff), however some knowledge of the dynamics can be useful if serious problems arise. Facilitate situations where you get to (briefly) interact with her friends—offer lifts, encourage movie nights, and get to know their parents. This can be difficult when the last thing your daughter wants is her Mom or Dad invading her social space, so just be there in the background—provide the snacks and drive the car, but take a step back and don't force yourself on them. Supervise from afar, ideally so that they don't even realise you are there. Make sure her friends feel comfortable within your home (but don't rule it!) and you will end up knowing much more about what is going on in her life. Remember, when you're a teenager *your* parents are uncool, but other people's parents aren't necessarily! If you are a safe ear for your daughter's friends, hopefully their parents will be the same for her.

Of course social interaction amongst teens is in some ways quite different to when we were young. Remember those hours we spent on the phone (desperately trying to escape the earshot of our parents!) or grappling with torturously low Internet speeds to send email or maybe chat on AIM or Messenger? Things are obviously a lot more connected and accessible for teens these days and with this comes many great opportunities, but also some concerns. Social media and the Internet are an important part of our kid's lives now. Restricting access is nigh on impossible; for the most part, you are much better off trying to keep her use out in the open rather than driving it 'underground' by keeping her away from it completely. The Internet is a vast and scary space, all the more reason why it is vital that your teen learns how to function in it. Internet literacy is a life skill like any other. One way or another, your parents taught you or you learnt phone etiquette, right? This is really the same thing, just a bit more technical. Loosen the leash gradually, teach her how to use this tool safely and properly and do your very best to keep apace with the ever-changing trends!

2. Clothes.

The teenage years are all about finding yourself. No teenage girl should make it through her teenage years without having committing at least a few fashion crimes that she will later look back on and cringe at. These are the rites of passage that prepare us for adulthood and help us find out who we are and who we want to be. Teenage fashion is designed to confuse, disgust and concern us. If you want your daughter to grow into the kind of adult who respects and is proud of her body, demands respect from others, knows her limits and is empowered, the issue of "What should I allow her to wear?" is crucial. The thing to keep in mind is this: clothes are a legitimate medium for self-expression and experimentation. While it is true that we are all judged by what we wear and how we present ourselves, the more we empower our daughters to express themselves freely in this way, the more we create a world where people are judged by their actions and words rather than their dress.

Sure, you should make sure your daughter knows how to 'dress to impress' for a job interview and other formal occasions. But also make sure she knows that her outward appearance is not a measure of her self-worth. The more these two things—her self-worth and her appearance—are disconnected in her mind, the less likely she is to use her clothes as a way to impress others (boys, girls, her friends) and the more likely she is to use clothes as a way of letting her creativity shine or to choose practicality and comfort over 'fashion'. Yes, each family has different values about this, and that's fine. But think carefully about the message you are sending your daughter when you tell her "you aren't leaving the house dressed like that!" Aside from the inefficacy of this strategy (when has this ever worked!) it also implies that others' behaviour towards her is directly tied to her clothing—a dangerous message that we shouldn't subject our precious daughters to.

3. Relationships.

Crushes. Holding hands. A first kiss. Love? Sex?! This aspect of parenting a teenager can go from sweet and simple to complicated and emotional very quickly. One minute they're running away from each other in the playground and the next they're obsessing over every word, every glance. And unfortunately this is often the area of their life that you will hear the least about. Even parents who have been very open and communicative about the details of puberty, sex education and relationships may find that this just isn't something their daughter wants to share with them when it becomes reality. This is normal. All you can do is show that you're interested and try to get them to share with you the main events. The trick is to do this without applying undue pressure—you don't want your 13-year-old to feel weird if she hasn't kissed anyone yet! You also don't want to confine them to a default view of their sexuality—keep it vague when it comes to naming genders, don't assume anything and let them fill in the gaps for you when they're ready.

Be prepared for the fact that what they tell you they're up to and what they actually are up to might be very different. While it would be nice to live in a fantasy land where you don't have to think about this stuff, that is a dangerous and damaging attitude to take when it comes to what could be some of the most influential relationships of your daughter's teen years. A good way to approach it if you feel like you don't have the detail required to share all your worldly wisdom with your daughter, is to try to anticipate the kinds of issues she might be facing. For example, she might be feeling like she is being left behind by her friends, or is moving much faster than them; she might be worried about how to know if someone likes her and what to do to show someone she likes them; she might be confused about feelings she has towards friends, platonic or romantic; she might be worried about how a friend is being treated by their girlfriend or boyfriend; she might be considering have sex.

Having generalized discussions with you daughter about these issues—sexuality, crushes, being in love, relationship dynamics, respect, sexual health and consent—will help you to get your values across in a less threatening way than if you try too hard to relate it to her specific situation, especially if you're not quite sure what that is! Of course, if you have a daughter who likes to talk about this stuff, let her do it! Don't be embarrassed; don't shame her for her feelings, desires, worries and questions. Remember: teaching her self-respect is the best way to ensure that she is respected. Set clear boundaries and be clear about what you expect of her, but most of all empower her to make good decisions and support her when she fails to.

4. School Work.

So much of a teenager's life seems to revolve around school. They spend a lot of time there after all. And yet, if you ask most teenagers about the highlights and lowlights of their day, very rarely will the content be related to what they're learning in class. The social ins and outs of their daily life are a far greater preoccupation. For this reason, it can be hard to get them to focus on the stuff they really should be: their classes. Just ask any teacher! This isn't to say that teenagers don't want to learn—most are innately curious beings who have a sense of wonder about the world and their place in it (hidden, of course behind a veil of sarcasm, 'cool' and faked disinterest). But we have to be realistic. School can be a drag when your limited life experience makes it hard to connect the subjects you are being lectured about with your future and the real world. Even schools with the most stimulating teaching style have students who are disengaged and underperforming. Unfortunately, most teenagers don't have the capacity to appreciate the education they are receiving.

The best way to overcome this is to be involved with their education. In the teenage years, your involvement might have to come from a greater distance than it did in elementary school, but that doesn't mean it should be lesser. Ask questions, even if you don't get extensive answers. It shows you care and that what they are doing is important. Be alert to any problems they are having with a particular class and show them that you are willing to help them find ways to improve. Encourage (and if necessary, enforce) good study habits from the get-go. Make it a non-negotiable early on when they are less likely to argue over doing homework and it will hopefully become a habit. Remind them constantly of the big picture—their goals and hopes for the future, without putting undue pressure on them about what kind of career they should have. Even if you think the goals they have are unrealistic or ill suited to their personality or talents, having a dream is the motivator that will help them through those boring classes. If they don't have a dream that happens to neatly fit into a college or career path, you can still encourage their passions and use them as a 'carrot' to reward their best efforts in school.

5. Chores.

Remember when she used to follow you around, begging to help in the yard, use the vacuum cleaner or help you cook dinner? Now, most likely, the tiniest hint of work will see her vanishing in a flash!

Once again, every family has different expectations when it comes to chores. For some families, the assistance of kids in the running of a household is mandatory, in the sense that, with two parents working, without the kids' help, things would come to a complete standstill. For other families, the kids' help is less necessary, but the parents want to instil a work ethic and ensure that their kids have the skills to survive once they leave home. Be clear about which of these best fits your family's needs and allocate chores appropriately according to this. Make your expectations for each family member well-defined— that way they will see how much you are doing, how much any siblings are doing, and will be more likely to accept their tasks. The best way to ensure that she pitches in her fair share is to give her chores that directly relate to her own well-being, such as laundry, or being responsible for the family meal. If she doesn't do it, she will feel the consequences of not having clean clothes, or having the rest of the family on her case because they're hungry! Tie other tasks to the things she wants. Tell her she can only get a lift to soccer practice later in the week if she's washed the car. Or, turn the WiFi off for a set period of time, and it only comes back on when everyone's completed a (reasonable) set list of tasks. (This can be just as motivating for Internet-addicted parents!)

When she complains, don't give in and do it for her! She will try to make you think that it would be easier if you just did it yourself. Instead, make sure she knows how to do it, and then leave it up to her. It's hard, repetitive and frustrating, but unfortunately it really is the only way.

Conclusion: The Other Side of the Teenage Years.

It's a cliché, but it's a cliché for a reason: Your job is to parent yourself out of a job. You are not your child's best friend; you are her parent. There is lots of time to develop a friendship with your child, but adolescence is not the time. What they need most from you at this time is a parent and the many roles that encompasses. Sometimes it means being the 'bad cop', the 'life ruiner'; at other times it means being their safe place, their soft place to fall. Judging when to take on this role, when to push them and when to let things go is the main conundrum of parenthood. You won't always get it right, but the clearer you can be about how you choose to respond to their behaviour, the more likely you are to make decisions grounded in logic rather than the tumultuous emotions that these years can bring up. In doing so, the voice in their head that tells them right from wrong and keeps them on a healthy and fulfilling path will gradually stop being yours and instead become their own.

In order to achieve this, you need to set clear and reasonable boundaries that naturally evolve over time. What was suitable for your daughter last year might not be this year. Show her that you are willing to reconsider 'the rules' as she matures and demonstrates that she is able to act responsibly. A gradual loosening of the leash is the goal here. Don't expect her to suddenly cope with everything once she turns eighteen if you haven't prepared her in baby-steps along the way. Ideally, you will start giving her responsibility from birth, throughout childhood and the tween years—times where she is more likely to be eager to please you and less likely to rebel for the sake of it. With this foundation set, the process of re-drawing the boundaries in the teen years will make for much smoother sailing—she's used to a gradual upping of her rights and responsibilities and knows that more freedom will come if she shows she knows how to think and act appropriately.

At the end of the day, the vast majority of teenagers (aside from those with special needs or particularly difficult life circumstances) will secretly come to respect you for creating boundaries, even if they don't necessarily respect the boundaries themselves. So if you sometimes feel like choosing the path of least resistance, giving in and acting like your teen daughter's best friend, think of it this way: be her parent for now, and you might just gain a very special friend for life.

Made in the USA
Columbia, SC
02 March 2021